I'm More than the Preacher's Wife

Discovering the Real You While Wearing Multiple Hats

May God bless you today and always.

Sara Phillips

Sara Phillips
3/5/16

CROSSBOOKS

CrossBooks™
A Division of LifeWay
1663 Liberty Drive
Bloomington, IN 47403
www.crossbooks.com
Phone: 1-866-879-0502

© 2014 Sara Phillips. All rights reserved.

No part of this book may be reproduced, stored in a retrieval system, or transmitted by any means without the written permission of the author.

Scripture taken from the New King James Version. Copyright 1979, 1980, 1982 by Thomas Nelson, inc. Used by permission. All rights reserved.

Scripture taken from the King James Version of the Bible.

First published by CrossBooks 06/04/2014

ISBN: 978-1-4627-3748-2 (sc)
ISBN: 978-1-4627-3749-9 (e)

Library of Congress Control Number: 2014909322

Printed in the United States of America.

This book is printed on acid-free paper.

Any people depicted in stock imagery provided by Thinkstock are models, and such images are being used for illustrative purposes only.
Certain stock imagery © Thinkstock.

Because of the dynamic nature of the Internet, any web addresses or links contained in this book may have changed since publication and may no longer be valid. The views expressed in this work are solely those of the author and do not necessarily reflect the views of the publisher, and the publisher hereby disclaims any responsibility for them.

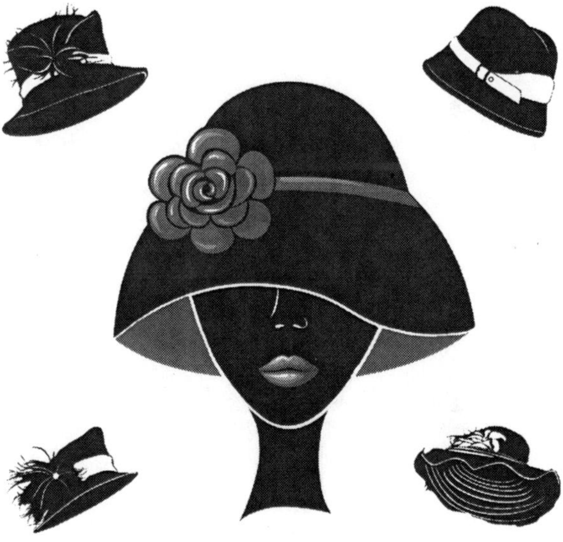

Contents

Acknowledgments and Special Thanks............. ix
Introduction xi
Chapter 1 The Role of the Preacher's Wife 1
Chapter 2 A Creation of God:
           Godly Characteristics 9
Chapter 3 Mirror, Mirror on the
           Wall: "Who Am I?" 17
Chapter 4 Help, I'm Drowning:
           Finding Balance 25
Chapter 5 Love Your Enemies:
           Dealing with Difficult People 35
Chapter 6 Walking in Your Calling................... 43
Chapter 7 I'm a Sheep Too! Feed Me,
           Lord, Feed Me!................................... 53
Chapter 8 Lord, Be Pleased! 61

Acknowledgments and Special Thanks

I would like to say a special thanks to my fellowship of first ladies, with whom I've been blessed to share friendship. It was through one of our Leading Ladies Luncheon planning sessions that I shared what God was depositing in my spirit. You definitely can identify with "In Her Shoes," a poem from my first book, *Treasures of the Heart: Poems Inspired by God.*

This book is dedicated to every first lady who shall travel this road. My prayer is that you discover many wonderful truths as you travel your own road as the preacher's wife. I've learned to be Sara, as that's all God intends, and He shall do the rest.

This book is in loving memory of First Lady Franconia M. Griffa, a precious jewel of God!

Introduction

"God is calling me into the ministry."

My husband's words changed my life. I felt such anxiety. *I've only been a wife for three years. I'm just learning to keep house, raise a family, and be a wife.* I was screaming inside. *Who's going to train me for this role? Can I even be a preacher's wife? What will be expected of me? Can I do this?* I began sobbing. *Lord, give me the strength!*

On February 4, 2001, my husband answered the call into the ministry. And I joined him.

Wives in ministry must wear multiple hats. These include, but are not limited to: woman, wife, mother, professional, friend, confidante, and preacher's wife. There are times when the thought of everything to be done is simply overwhelming, especially because on top of the many hats already mentioned, the church expects you to wear an entirely different list of hats, including singer, Sunday school teacher, youth advisor, missionary, counselor, and secretary. God has given every preacher's wife her own hats to wear. We do not all wear the same hats, but the hats we do wear are many.

This book was birthed from one of my poems called "I'm More Than the Preacher's Wife." It was written during a time when I was attempting to figure out this role of preacher's wife. Let me share it with you.

I'm More Than the Preachers Wife!

I'm more than the preacher's wife!
I'm an anointed woman,
a willing instrument to be used by God.
I have a career and a family. I have a life!
I'm more than the preacher's wife.

A preacher's wife is not a role or a crown to be worn.
It is a calling that God adorns.
You're called to visit the sick,
Called to pray for the bereaved,
Called to minister to the young ladies in the church,
Called to serve the congregation in humility.
You're called to teach Bible study,
Called to teach Sunday school,
Called to work with the youth in the church.

You're called to be the secretary for the pastor.
You may even be called to lead the women's ministry at church.

You're called to assist your husband with counseling.
You're called to love those who don't love you back.
You're called to sacrifice your life for the ministry.
That's the life for a preacher's wife!

Outside of all of those responsibilities,
You're also called to hold down a career to help support the family.
You're expected to have the house kept and the Dinner prepared when your husband gets home.
You're called to minister to your husband to keep Him encouraged—my, so many hats "you" must wear!

You're called out by God to serve the ministry,
Alongside the preacher as his wife!
Many have been chosen, but only a few are called!

Proverbs 3:13–18 states:

> Happy is the man who finds wisdom, and the man who gains understanding; for her proceeds are better than the profits of silver, and her gain than fine gold. She is more precious than rubies, and all the things you may desire cannot compare with her. Length of days is in her right hand, in her left hand riches and honor. Her ways are ways of pleasantness, and all her paths are peace. She is a tree of life to those who take hold of her, and happy are all who retain her.

Knowledge is power; therefore, we must all obtain knowledge. Your walk as a preacher's wife will be unique to you. Writing this book is my attempt to share my story and knowledge with other first ladies destined to travel this road.

Chapter 1

The Role of the Preacher's Wife

A preacher's wife is not a role or a crown to be worn.
It is a calling that God adorns.
 ~ From "I'm More Than a Preacher's Wife"

Dress modestly.
Be pleasant.
Smile.
Be qualified to teach any age.
Sing or play the piano.
Make sure the house is always ready for company.

When my husband accepted the call into the ministry, I immediately recalled the common list of preacher's-wife requirements I had heard all my life. Despite this long list of qualities a preacher's wife is supposed to possess, the items not on the list, those that were totally unknown and became surprises, were the items that caused me the most anxiety. *Lord, can I possibly fill all those expectations?*

Six years after my husband's initial call to the ministry, he accepted the call to be a pastor. I knew God was using him and moving him into places of leadership where He wanted him to serve. At the time, I was attending sessions with other ministers' wives, but nothing completely prepared me for the role of preacher's wife.

Everyone has an idea of what the preacher's wife is supposed to do.

"Oh, no. The preacher's wife always sits on *this* pew." (That comment was always accompanied by a pointing finger.)

"Good morning. That outfit is really not suitable for the preacher's wife. Don't you have anything else to wear?"

"It seems to me you should have spoken up to our women's ministry committee."

"Mrs. Preacher, you really shouldn't spend your time with *that* group of women. They don't always agree with your husband."

My prayer was always, *Lord, I just want to serve You. I just want to come worship with others who love You. Please have these people accept me as I am.*

As I prepared to step into the role of preacher's wife, and as the time for my husband to be installed as pastor came closer, I became more anxious. Yes, the role of preacher's wife frightened me! Not only was *I* pressured, but my husband was also getting advice about what I should be doing. There were so many hats to wear—literally.

However, as I look back on my short time as a preacher's wife, I realize that remembering a few things made my life more manageable.

1. I am a creation of God first—an instrument that God chose to use.
2. I am not the pastor in my husband's absence. God called *him* as the shepherd.
3. I am a sheep and I too need a shepherd.
4. My primary role is to care for my spouse and our family, to provide a peaceful and nurturing home.
5. I can't be all things to all people. I must seek to fulfill the will of God.

God knew how inadequate I felt in fulfilling this role, so He revealed these nuggets to remind me of my worth in Him. God ordains and aligns things the way He desires. Even though I didn't feel equipped, God chose me as His instrument.

God creates each of us with a purpose. My purpose is not your purpose, and vice versa. Do what God has ordained you to do! If you don't know what your purpose is yet, seek God sincerely for your path.

Romans 8:28–31 says:

And know that all things work together for the good to those who love God, to those who are called according to his purpose. For whom he foreknew, he also predestined to be conformed to the image of his Son, that he might be the firstborn among many brethren. Moreover whom he predestined, them he also called; whom he called, these he also justified; and whom he justified; those he also glorified. What then shall we say to these things? If God is for us, who can be against us?

In April 2008, my husband was installed as pastor. As he and I entered the church, I walked in knowing that God had purposed that day. Regardless of what I faced in the role of preacher's wife, God would always be right there with me.

Reflections...

Do you feel your past training/workshops prepared you for your call to be an effective minister's wife?

_____

_____

_____

Do you have a close friend/ministry wife who can guide/mentor you? Can you confide in her?

_____

_____

_____

Prayer:

> *Lord, thank you for creating us to be unique and special people. I know it was by Your hands we were fashioned and by Your power we exist. God, help us to understand that it's okay to be ourselves. God, grant us the strength and ability to do all You have placed in us to complete. If You see that we're lacking anything, please, God, impart it to*

us that we may better serve You and Your people. We love, honor, adore, and thank You for our Savior, Jesus Christ, who died that we may live. Thank You for that awesome sacrifice given to redeem all of mankind. Amen.

Chapter 2

A Creation of God: Godly Characteristics

I will praise you, for I am fearfully and wonderfully made Marvelous are your works, and that my soul knows very well.

~Psalm 139:14

God formed me in my mother's womb and breathed life into me. God charted my path before it was revealed to me, to my spouse, or to the church. God planned for me to be the one to stand next to the man He called into ministry, and He fashioned me for that purpose.

The first godly characteristic a preacher's wife should develop is a humble spirit. She should be willing to submit and to sacrifice. Every preacher's wife must be willing to share her pastor husband with three hundred to four hundred other people.

Learning to be a wife who is a support system, and not a stumbling block to God's plan and purpose, is important. As the preacher's family, your family is a witness for God in a unique way. Yes, being the family of a preacher involves great sacrifice, but I believe God expects our family relationships to be an example to our congregations. Your family schedule and dynamics may be unique, but so are those of a doctor, policeman, or nurse, for example.

There will be nights when your plans must be placed on the back burner. Your husband may miss special dates, activities, and sporting events for your children, and you will still be responsible for explaining to them why their father is not there. There may be periods when you feel totally alone with all the responsibilities.

The second characteristic a preacher's wife needs is a servant's heart. Matthew 20:26–28 states:

> Yet it shall not be so among you; but whoever desires to become great among you, let him be your servant. And whoever desires to be first among you, let him be your slave—just as the Son of Man did not come to be served, but to serve, and to give His life a ransom for many.

We have not come to be served, but to serve! You must be willing to exalt others above yourself, considering and preferring them over yourself. You serve the congregation as unto God. You assist the pastor with visiting the sick and grieved members of the church. Although there will be times when you don't quite feel capable, know that God has equipped you in all areas needed to serve the congregation. My prayer is this: "Not my will but let thy will be done."

The third characteristic you must have is a rich prayer life. Sometimes the only person you can confide in is God. God has placed you as the pastor's mate, so you share the things that weigh heavily on his heart. That requires wisdom and understanding that can only come from God. Much of the time, you will not be privy to all the information; however, it is important to seek God in prayer, asking that He who sees all will answer and deliver. Intercede for your spouse, family, and congregation. God has called you to be a strong tower and prayer warrior for your family, spouse, and church family. Carry all of your burdens to the altar of God, and leave them there. As Scripture states:

> Be anxious for nothing, but in everything by prayer and supplication, with thanksgiving, let your requests be made known to God; and the peace of God, which surpasses all understanding, will guard your hearts and minds through Christ Jesus (Philippians 4:6, 7).

Therefore humble yourselves under the mighty hand of God, that He may exalt you in due time, casting all your care upon Him, for He cares for you (1 Peter 5:6, 7).

Prayer is the main source of communication with God the Father. Your prayer life should be consistent, without wavering. Pray for God's will to be done, regardless of the situation, and trust God knows what is best for you, your spouse, and your church family.

Reflections...

What characteristics has God given you?

_____

_____

_____

Seek godly friends and women with whom you can share your heart. Do you currently have godly women with whom you can share your heart?

_____

_____

_____

Prayer:

> *God, I thank you for allowing me to serve you and your people. Always be my focus, and extend your grace and mercy to your people through me. Help me to be supportive, loving, submissive, humble, and kind. Help me to be a willing prayer warrior. Each day, give me the strength and desire to walk worthy of my calling. "Let the words of*

my mouth and the meditation of my heart be acceptable in your sight, O Lord, my strength and my redeemer" (Psalm 19:14). It's in Jesus' name that I pray and ask it all.

Chapter 3

Mirror, Mirror on the Wall: "Who Am I?"

But we all, with unveiled face, beholding as in a mirror the glory of the Lord, are being transformed into the same image from glory to glory, just as by the Spirit of the Lord.

~2 Corinthians 3:18

One Saturday afternoon, I was cleaning my bathroom. I sprayed Windex on the not-so-clear mirror. When I wiped away the cloudy haze, the mirror became clear. As I looked in the mirror, I did not recognize the person starring back at me. *Who am I?* I wondered.

I had been attempting, as a young minister's wife, to cross every *t* and dot every *i*. I was seeking to meet all of the expectations placed on me. I consented to whatever I was asked to do, as I did not want to disappoint my husband or the church family. I did not have any training, and I felt so unprepared for this journey.

I stood in front of the mirror for a minute or two longer, and the question resurfaced: *Who are you?*

I couldn't answer that question, nor did I realize when this change took place that made me not recognize the person staring back at me in the mirror.

My name is Sara, and I'm a child of God! Just then, Jeremiah 1:5 came to mind. It says, "Before I formed you in the womb I knew you; before you were born I sanctified you." At that moment, I wanted to find the answer to the question, "Who am I?"

My mother named me after my grandmother, Sarah Geneale; however, during that time, many children were given biblical names. As I began to research the biblical meaning, I discovered *Sara* means "woman of high ranking," and it is translated as "princess," pure and happy. Other sources indicated that *Sara* means "a person who has a deep inner desire for love and companionship and strives to work with others to achieve peace and harmony."

My research further stated that people with the name Sara are people who tend to be quiet, cooperative, considerate, and sympathetic to others—adaptable, balanced, and sometimes shy. They are trustworthy and respect the confidence of others. They are often very intuitive. They like detail and order and often find change worrisome. They may sometimes feel insecure or restless, according to http://www.sheknows.com/baby-names/name/sarah assessed November 23, 2013.

I felt great as I began to get reacquainted with myself. The name *Sara* biblically means princess, lady pure and happy. I should not be sad or feel that I'm not what everyone else expects me to be. I was created by God. As I read the various words that describe me, I could see myself:

- sympathetic to others
- likes detail and order
- considerate
- trustworthy
- sometimes insecure and restless
- has a deep desire for love and companionship

God, is it okay if I feel unprepared as a minister's wife? Thank you, Lord. Now I understand how You carefully crafted me during my creation.

It was a joy to know God created me, fashioned me, and equipped me for this journey. I am what He says that I am, and I can accomplish what God has placed in my hands to do. Psalm 139:13–14 states:

> For you formed my inward parts; you covered me in my mother's womb. I will praise you, for I am fearfully and wonderfully made; marvelous are your works, and that my soul knows very well.

Everything that God makes is good, and that includes me. So… who am I? I'm Sara, child of the highest God and King. I am the head and not the tail. I am above and not beneath. I am fearfully and wonderfully made! It's okay to be me!

Who am I? I'm more than the preacher's wife! I am a unique creation by God.

- I am fearfully and wonderfully made.
- I am a mother.
- I am a wife.
- I am a daughter.
- I am a professional, and I have a career.
- I am in awe that God chose me as His instrument.

Reflections…

Have you lost your sense of direction during your transition to being a minister's wife?

_____

_____

_____

What are you willing to do to regain your ground?

_____

_____

_____

Prayer:

> *God, we thank You for Your creation as You remind us that everything You make is good, and that includes us. Lord, we acknowledge that You're aware of our beginning and ending. There is nothing that escapes You, and therefore, we look to You as we seek to follow your purpose and plan for our lives. What a loving, compassionate, merciful, gracious, and kind Father You are. There is nothing that we*

encounter that You have not already ordained and orchestrated. Your Word says that You shall never leave nor forsake us. Thank You for being a shield of protection for us. Thank You, Lord, that when we lose our sense of direction, You kindly lead us back on the path and journey You have for us. We give Your name the honor and the glory for the great things You have done. Amen.

Chapter 4

Help, I'm Drowning: Finding Balance

Take my yoke upon you and learn from Me, for I and gentle and lowly in heart, and you will find rest for your souls. For my yoke is easy and my burden is light.

~Matthew 11:29–30

When I was a child, I never learned to swim. I recall almost drowning during a summer camp experience. My hands were flailing, my feet were kicking, and panic overcame me. I couldn't find my way to the top of the water. I was afraid I was going to die. *Where is everybody else?*

The lifeguard rescued me. Excess water was pumped from my insides, causing me to choke and sputter—my most vivid memory!

The demands placed on a minister's wife are similar to my experience with drowning. I was attempting to be a mother, wife, preacher's wife, friend, and confidante, as well as trying to have my own career in banking. I cared for the congregation but struggled to find time to minister to them. "There was no way I could live up to the expectations people had for a minister's wife." I felt the waters of life closing in on me.

Every day, the struggle to keep my head above the water is greater, and I sink a little lower. I'm going down. I'm so busy doing everything possible to fill the gaps in my life, how can I effectively fulfill all of the responsibilities on my plate?

Matthew 9:37–38 says, "Then he said to his disciples, 'The harvest is plentiful but the labors are few. Therefore pray the Lord of the harvest to send laborers into his harvest.'"

It is perceived that the preacher's wife should be gifted in all areas and able to step in at a moment's notice and perform perfectly. Can someone please give me a copy of the preacher's wife manual?

Unrealistic expectations—where do they come from? They come from years and years of society saying what a preacher's wife should be. Expectations come from everywhere: my congregation, my spouse, and other ministry wives. As a preacher's wife, I am constantly compared to previous ministry wives. I am expected to be at every church service, Bible study, and Sunday school session—no questions asked.

On top of that, I am expected to be dressed appropriately. "This differs from congregation to congregation, but there are always expectations" even if you don't have the resources to make this possible. But God does not look at our outside appearances. God looks at the intents of our hearts.

The word *no* was not in my vocabulary. It was like I was starting a new career with seasoned employees all around me. I felt like I had to do everything in my power to prove to the boss that he made the right decision in hiring me. As a new ministry wife, I wanted to be accepted and do what was required of me. I did not count on being burned out by all of those expectations.

God's Word says, "And let us not grow weary while doing good, for in due season we shall reap if we do not lose heart. Therefore, as we have the opportunity, let us do good to all, especially to those who are of the household of faith" (Galatians 6:9–10). And the great commission says we should teach the Word of God to all that come to the knowledge of God. As I have the opportunity, I should always seek to do good to all and share God's Word, but I am *not* supposed to be all to all. I can serve the Lord only in the in areas which He has equipped and prepared me. In order to save myself from drowning, I had to shed some of my current responsibilities.

My primary role was to take care of my family, husband, and home. God will never put more on us than we're able to bear, but we tend to overextend ourselves to the point of exhaustion.

Finding balance involves setting healthy boundaries for yourself, your spouse, and the church. If you're still working outside (or inside) of the home, it's okay to say, "I'm sorry, my schedule has no vacancies right now," or, "Thank you for considering me, but I'm unavailable at this time." Finding harmony and peace within your schedule is essential. As I said, you can't be all to all. And God has provided all that's needed from within His congregation.

It's also important to know your abilities and limitations. If ushering causes you to have an unpleasant demeanor because you have issues with standing for a two-and-a-half-hour Sunday morning service, you should not participate in that ministry.

I can't tell you how important it is to know your limits. Remember, you still have a career, children, a spouse, and a church family. Each is important and requires your attention.

When our daughter was younger, she was involved in Girl Scouts and sporting events. Her father often had church meetings, so I made sure I was there to provide her the support she needed. There were also a few times when I could not get away from work, so my husband was there to support the children.

The pastor and his wife are always on duty. Therefore, both should be available when a need in the congregation arises. The process of shedding some of my responsibilities was a little unsettling for me (and our congregation) in the beginning, but it was necessary for me to take care of my family, to be available to the congregation, and for my own spiritual growth.

Reflections…

Have you become burned out by all of the expectations on a minister's wife?

_____

_____

_____

Do you often feel guilty when you're unable to be at every church service?

_____

_____

_____

Prayer:

Lord, please give me a servant's heart that I may serve You and do my part. Impart to me Your kindness and love that I may share with all those I come in contact with. Give me an encouraging word that I might say and a prayer that reaches Your ears. Help my life to be a light in darkness and my thoughts to be pure before You. If I should fall along the way, forgive me of my sins and send me quickly on my way. God, help me to be a minister's wife You can be pleased with and a willing vessel in which Your Spirit can reside. Amen.

Chapter 5

Love Your Enemies: Dealing with Difficult People

You have heard that it was said, You shall love your neighbor and hate your enemies; But I say unto you, Love your enemies, bless those who curse you, do good to those who hate you, and pray for those who spitefully use you and persecute you, that you may be sons of your Father in Heaven; for He makes His sun rise on the evil and on the good, and sends rain on the just and on the unjust.

~Matthew 5:43–45

Dealing with conflict and difficult people is part of serving in ministry. You will be persecuted and disliked simply because God has chosen you to stand beside and encourage your husband as he makes decisions—many that will not be popular with people in the congregation. God assigned your husband to be the shepherd of the flock, to provide direction and instruction to the entire body. He has a huge responsibility on his shoulders. Disagreements will happen, and someone is going to be offended at some time. Conflict is unavoidable, so you must learn how to deal with it and the difficult people who are the offenders or the offended.

Criticism about those you love is hard to bear. When you hear critical talk about your pastor husband, it is easy to get discouraged. Part of your job as the pastor's wife is to be loving and supportive of your husband while still loving the congregation unconditionally. And when one or both of you is criticized, you must never let the enemy tempt you to become defensive.

Criticism affects both you and your husband, because you are a team. Do not be discouraged;

you are not the first minister's wife to encounter conflict, persecution, adversity, and yes, even some hostility. Ministry does not exempt you from conflicts and disagreements, so you must learn to seek God for wisdom in how to handle each situation.

The enemy will assign storms and trials to you. For every new level of purpose and responsibility you have, the Devil or another of his adversaries is waiting to discourage, trap, and oppose you and your God-given ministry. For every new revelation, there is a new challenge. And nothing adequately prepares us for the difficult people and situations we encounter on this journey. However, we can seek God for wisdom on how to love every person in the congregation effectively.

Matthew 5:7 says, "Blessed are the merciful for they shall obtain mercy." Difficult people are sent into our lives to produce some things in us: patience, insight, sensitivity, humility, and perseverance. The race is not given to the swift or to the strong but to those who endure to the end.

Remember, we don't have to do it in our own strength. God will help us love the unlovable!

Psalm 46:1, 5 encourages, "God is our refuge and our strength a very present help in trouble. Even though the earth be removed, and though the mountains be carried in the midst of the sea… God is in the midst of her and she shall not be moved." God is in the midst of our lives, and He has ordained for us to stand, knowing that He is our hiding place. Psalm 32:7 states, "You are my hiding place; you shall preserve me from trouble; you shall surround me with songs of deliverance. Selah."

God also shall keep us from falling into the various traps that the enemy sets for us. Psalm 37:23 says, "The steps of a good man are ordered by the Lord, and He delights in his way, though he fall, he shall not be utterly cast down; For the Lord upholds him with His hand."

There is an appointed end to the trials and storms we face. John 16:33 says, "These things I have spoken to you, that in Me you may have peace. In the world you will have tribulation; but be of good cheer, I have overcome the world." We have a God who already overcame every trial in which we could find ourselves, and we can stand in confidence because we know that God will not put more on us then we are able to bear. When we are tempted, He will make a way of escape that we may be able to bear it (1 Cor. 10:13).

Can you love your enemies? Can you love those who use you, persecute you, and falsely say all manner of evil against you for Christ's sake? Jesus declares that you can and that He has given each of us the strength to endure whatever trial or storm we find ourselves in. Why? First Peter 4:8 says, above all things, have fervent love for one another, for "love will cover a multitude of sins."

Reflections...

How do you deal with disagreements with members in the church?

_____

_____

_____

What are some other challenges you face with the membership?

_____

_____

_____

Prayer:

> *God, thank You for reminding me that You are the source of everything I need and that all I need to do is seek You and I shall find You. You are my secret place and tabernacle, where I can hide from all the attacks forged against me.*
>
> *In Matthew 5:9–10, it says, "Blessed are the peacemakers, for they shall be called sons of*

God. Blessed are those who are persecuted for righteousness sake, for theirs is the kingdom of heaven." God, I know when I stand on Your Word that persecution and adversity will come. However, I'm thankful that when I face adversity from mankind, I can find peace in You.

I thank You for Jesus Christ, who was persecuted for all people. He took on my sins so that I can be reconciled back to You. Thank You for giving me a spirit willing to live at peace with all people. Regardless of what trials I face in this life, I know that You shall be there with me to see me through to the end of my journey. We love, honor, and adore You. In Jesus' name, we pray. Amen.

Chapter 6

Walking in Your Calling

Trust in the Lord with all your heart, And lean not on your own understanding; In all your ways acknowledge Him, And He shall direct your paths.

~Proverbs 3:5, 6

The preacher's wife is the shadow of the man who preaches every Sunday morning, but she also has her own calling. I am thankful God chose my husband to fill the pulpit as the shepherd of the church who serves and tends to the sheep: God's people. I am also thankful He chose me to be the wife of a preacher.

There are times, however, when I wish that we had more normal lives. Some think this is a glamorous walk of fame, and many are caught up in the role of first lady of the church, who even gets to sit in the front row in some churches. But ministers' wives are human too. We have feelings, and there will be times when we must put the needs of our families above the needs of the church. When that happens, you don't have to feel guilty. God has called you to wear multiple hats. You are a mother and must nurture and shield your children from conflicts and church business while attempting to maintain a level of normalcy. You are a wife, and you must encourage your husband and be that strong shoulder for him to lean on. You must learn to be a master multitasker who is able to juggle and manage lengthy calendars.

All Christians were crafted and created by God with a purpose and a plan. And even though pastors' wives don't pastor a congregation, all believers are ministers of God's Word. We all have the responsibility to study and apply God's words to our lives.

Only God knows what work He has called you to do. Yes, you have a calling as well. The charge is given to the pastor to shepherd the flock, to lead God's people. And God has gifted and anointed you for a specific work too. Walk in your calling, fulfill your purpose, and understand that your destiny will not be an exact match to the previous minister's wife.

> Trust in the Lord with all your heart, And lean not on your own understanding; In all your ways acknowledge Him, And He shall direct your paths (Proverbs 3:5, 6).

Seek God for his guidance and direction, for He shall lead you down the path created for you. Pray for God's will to be revealed in your life. And pray as David did: "Search me, oh God, and know my heart; try me, and know my anxieties" (Psalm 139:23).

The process of walking in your calling will not be easy. You will sometimes feel anxious and occasionally doubt your abilities. You cannot allow this to keep you from walking in your calling. The work God is calling you to do cannot be fulfilled by someone else; only you can fill those shoes.

Walk with assurance that God has gifted you; walk with confidence. You are an anointed woman of God. Walk with the power and authority placed in you to complete your calling. Walk knowing that if you fall, you serve a God who is able to pick you up and restore your joy. Walk knowing that you are not alone. In your weakness, you are also strong. Walk in your calling, you mighty woman of God!

"In Her Shoes"

Who can measure the steps she takes? Who can value the gestures she makes?

She is the lady God chose to stand next to the man He called. She has broad shoulders on which he has to lean.

She has a smile to cover all the pain they encounter. She is his eyes. She sees danger coming from afar and begins to intercede for her husband and family in prayer.

She wipes away the tears from his eyes after the world has beaten him down. Her presence and support give him strength to endure.

Who can measure the steps she takes? Who can value the gestures she makes? Only another who walks in her shoes.

She's well-spoken, classy, strong, and an anointed woman of God! Her words are seasoned with the preparation of the Word of God and the Holy Spirit.

She will always be there when all others walk away, so you see, not all can walk in her shoes. Why? Because she is God's leading lady.

Reflections...

Have you taken time to discover what you were called to do?

_____

_____

_____

Are you seeking God for your purpose? What is preventing you from listening to God?

_____

_____

_____

Prayer:

> *God, thank You for creating me. It was by Your power that I came to be. What love You must have had when You fashioned me. I understand that I'm fearfully and wonderfully made in Your image, and everything that You make is good. Even though I've had a long journey to endure, with high mountains and low valleys, You were*

right there in the midst of them with me. If I had a thousand tongues, I could not thank You enough for when You carried me. Lord, when I was sick, You healed me, and when I was of low estate, You encouraged me. Just when I wanted to give up, I felt Your loving arms comforting me. I'm the jewel that You created, and I'm okay just being me. Lord, thank You again for creating me. Amen.

Chapter 7

I'm a Sheep Too! Feed Me, Lord, Feed Me!

Study to shew thyself approved unto God, a workman that needeth not to be ashamed, rightly dividing the word of truth.

~2 Timothy 2:15 KJV

But he answered, and said, "It is written, man shall not live by bread alone but by every word that proceeds from the mouth of God" (Matthew 4:4).

I was caught at a crossroads as a ministry wife who was attempting to satisfy all the requirements placed on me. I was so busy that I could not focus on my purpose and God's plan for me. I felt so inadequate at this point in my journey. Even though I was humbly seeking to serve God and His people the best that I could, it appeared I was not getting a passing grade on my ministry wife report card.

Then I realized that I was a starving sheep. I was giving all to all and was spiritually malnourished. I am a sheep who needs a shepherd. It may be shocking for a ministry wife to say she's a sheep. But I'm a child of God, and therefore, I need to be filled with His Holy Spirit too. Just like everyone else, I need to feed on the Word of God. The Word of God changes the lives of all Christians. My salvation is just as important to me as any other Christian's is to him or her. And our primary role as sheep is to get fed so we can be equipped for the service God has called us to.

I cried out to God, "Feed me, Lord, feed me!"

God answered, *"I never told you to do all those things! I told you in Matthew 6:33 to 'Seek ye first the kingdom of God and its righteousness and then all else will be added unto you.'*

"I see that you've fed my sheep, but when was the last time you've eaten and feasted on My Word for your growth and development?"

I hung my head. My focus had not been on my purpose for a long time! I knew I had to act on that revelation from God.

God empowered me and granted me another opportunity to get to where He desired me to be. He has been too good to me! My obedience to God was essential to move forward on this journey.

Second Timothy 2:15 says, "Study to shew thyself approved unto God, a workman that neededth not to be ashamed, rightly dividing the word of truth." I knew that my spirit was empty and needed to be replenished, so I decided to take some much-needed time to focus on my personal spiritual growth and development.

During this period, God began to reveal part of my purpose: writing. This was truly an awakening for me. I never knew God intended for me to be an author. I knew there must be some purpose for my being; I just wasn't sure what it was. But as I began to pray, read, and listen to God, parts of my destiny were revealed unto me.

> Blessed are those who hunger and thirst for righteousness for they shall be filled (Matthew 5:6).

Reflections…

Is your spiritual bank low?

_____

_____

_____

What steps are you taking to ensure that you continue to grow and develop in the Lord?

_____

_____

_____

Prayer:

Lord, Your Word says, "Blessed are those who hunger and thirst for righteousness for they shall be fed." God, I thank You because with You, all things are possible. Even when I feel that I've reached the end of my abilities, You extend to me more mercy and grace. And what You provide is sufficient for this journey.

Thank You for my church family and for teaching me to be a meek, loving, serving, and praying vessel. Lord, help me to find balance in my life so that I can effectively serve You and Your kingdom. Give me the courage to say no when I've reached my limits, and allow me to be obedient to Your lead. Let my light so shine that Your goodness and grace will be evident in my life.

Chapter 8

Lord, Be Pleased!

By this I know that you are well pleased with me, Because my enemy does not triumph over me.

~Psalm 41:11

Lord, let not my living be in vain and all my decisions unexplained, Lord please show me the way.

~Sara Phillips
Treasures of the Heart,
Poems Inspired by God

At some point, we must give thought to our final resting places. We have to ask ourselves, "Have I done as God ordained for me to do? Will I be welcomed into the kingdom of God after I stand before my judge? Am I the disciple God intended me to be? Is God pleased with me?"

We want people to acknowledge, encourage, approve, and back our choices in life. Sometimes we discover we don't measure up to their standards. A little something extra is required for us to be accepted by them and the world.

Throughout His entire ministry, Jesus sought to minister to people right where they were. He never insisted that they be completely clean before He accepted them. He looked at their hearts and responded to their faith. Once He restored them, He often told them, "Go; your faith has made you whole… tell no one."

Jesus never looked for the approval or acknowledgement of anyone other than God the Father. He was sent by God to be the Savior of the world, and He never deviated from the purpose God orchestrated for Him. Even during His suffering on the cross, Jesus completed his assignment.

Prior to ascending to heaven, Jesus said, "Go therefore and make disciples of all the nations, baptizing them in the name of the Father and of the Son and of the Holy Spirit, teaching them to observe all things that I have commanded you; and lo, I am with you always, even to the end of the age. Amen" (Matthew 28:19–20).

Is God pleased with me? I certainly would like for Him to be pleased with me and the efforts I make on this journey.

Over the years, I have learned something very important: as long as I seek to follow His instructions, yes, God will be pleased with me! At the end of the day, I want to hear God say, "Well done, thy good and faithful servant!"

Seeking the acknowledgement, encouragement, and approval of others in life is good. However, it is not without conditions. Christians are supposed to encourage and uplift one another. I am my sister's keeper. Our God created us all to be unique and different, filled with His purpose. God loves us unconditionally, with all of our faults and inadequacies. And He wants us to use everything we have and are to serve and glorify Him.

> Therefore, my beloved brethren, be steadfast, immovable, always abounding in the work of the Lord, knowing that your labor is not in vain in the Lord (1 Corinthians 15:58).

After I researched my name, Sara, I became reacquainted with the jewel that God created me to be. God allowed me to wear many hats: woman, wife, mother, aunt, friend, confidant, and preacher's wife. At each place, He equipped me to be the person He desired me to be, with every detail carefully embedded! Although there were stumbling blocks along the way, I continued to trust God. He stated He will always be with us, and He always keeps His promises.

Keep trusting Him to be your strength and provide all you need. He created you as a precious jewel too, and He has a special plan for you. Follow Him, obey Him, trust Him, love and glorify Him with your life, and He will be pleased.

> Therefore humble yourselves under the mighty hand of God, that he may exalt you in due time (1 Peter 5:6).

Reflections...

Seek God to ensure that you're on the right path. In what areas do you feel you need to improve?

_____

_____

_____

Prayer:

Lord, thy Word is a lamp unto our feet and a light unto our paths. We know that there is nothing You shall withhold from us. Teach us Your Word and equip us that we may better serve You. Show us our sins that we may repent and return to right standing with You. Help me to be the minister's wife You will be pleased with. In Jesus' name, we pray. Amen.

There Is More to Me Than You See

There's more to me than you see!
You see an ordinary being, unsure of what I shall
Become or be.
There were even times when I couldn't see what
You were doing in me.

We should never judge a book by its cover.
Take the time to open the book, study its contents;
Get to know me.
As you discover and read of my journey, you will
Understand my pain, my suffering, my tears, my
Loneliness, my depression, my love.
You shall truly get to know me!

You'll understand what moves me.
The things that cause me joy.
Then, and only then, can you discover the jewel
God created—me.
The love God had when He fashioned me.

Lord, although many could not see what You were
Doing in me.
I'm so thankful that You decided to fashion, form,

Create, and breathe the breath of life in me.
For You caused me to be.
There is so much more to me than many can see.

"For I know the thoughts that I think toward you," says the Lord, "thoughts of peace and not of evil, to give you a future and a hope" (Jeremiah 29:11).